MAKE YOUR OWN
CUTTING BOARDS

SMART PROJECTS *and* **STYLISH DESIGNS** *for a* **HANDS-ON KITCHEN**

MAKE YOUR OWN
CUTTING BOARDS

SMART PROJECTS *and* STYLISH DESIGNS *for a* HANDS-ON KITCHEN

DAVID PICCIUTO

SPRING HOUSE PRESS

Publisher: Paul McGahren
Editorial Director: Matthew Teague
Copy Editor: Kerri Grzybicki
Design: Lindsay Hess
Layout: Michael Douglas
Illustration: Michael Douglas
Project and Cover Photography: Danielle Atkins
Step-by-Step Photography: David Picciuto & Eric Oblander

Spring House Press
P.O. Box 239
Whites Creek, TN 37189

ISBN: 978-1-940611-45-7
Library of Congress Control Number: 2016955782
Printed in the United States of America
Second Printing: August 2017

Note:
The following list contains names used in *Making Your Own
Cutting Boards* that may be registered with the United States
Copyright Office:
Apple iPad; BESSEY; BLACK+DECKER; Bosch; Buckeye Beer;
Denali; Drunken Woodworker; Everbilt; Facebook; Festool;
Fine Woodworking; Fitbit; Grizzly Industrial; Instagram; KenCraft;
Laura Lee Balanced; Le Trou Du Diable; Les Quatre Surfeurs
de L'Apocalypso; Make Something; Maumee Bay Brewing Co.;
MICROJIG GRR-RIPPER 3D Pushblock; Minwax; Patreon;
Rockler; Rockwell ShopSeries; SawStop; Sharpie; Sony;
Titebond; Twitter; YouTube

To learn more about Spring House Press books, or to find
a retailer near you, email *info@springhousepress.com*
or visit us at *www.springhousepress.com*.

CONTENTS

INTRODUCTION

Ask a woodworker if they've made a cutting board and nearly all of them will say they have in the past and still do to this day. For many it's their first woodworking project. For others it's their go-to project when they're looking for an excuse to get into the shop. Every kitchen needs a cutting board and nearly every shop is equipped to make them.

Cutting boards can be as simple as a single board or contain dozens of pieces with multiple species and shapes. Some require very few tools and others require a whole shop full of tools. The beauty of cutting boards is that no matter what your skill level or how many tools you have, you can make cutting boards—beautiful, useful cutting boards, to boot.

I got started in making cutting boards a few years ago when I was getting ready for a local craft show. When trying to sell my handmade items at shows I encourage potential buyers to touch them and pick them up. I want them to feel the quality and weight.

Selling cutting boards at craft fairs can be a great way to make some extra cash to buy that new tool or to get some of the fancy wood you've had your eye on. Making cutting boards can also be a great way to make handmade gifts for your friends and family. Or it might just be a good way to transform scrap wood into something useful for your own kitchen.

Whether you're an experienced woodworker or just starting out, I hope you find a new technique in this book that you can add to your skill set. More importantly I hope you can find inspiration in the shapes and designs and use it to come up with your own style. You are free to make any of the cutting boards found in this book and sell them for profit.

Who the heck am I? I'm a full-time blogger and YouTuber on a mission to inspire, entertain, and encourage. I believe everyone has the ability to be creative if they search for it within themselves.

David Picciuto
Make Something

Website — www.MakeSomething.tv
YouTube — www.youtube.com/MakeSomething
Twitter — www.twitter.com/drunkenwood
Facebook — www.facebook.com/MakeSomethingTV
Instagram — www.instagram.com/MakeSomethingTV

LIVE EDGE

Bring the feel of nature to the kitchen

TOOLS & SUPPLIES

› Chisel
› Mallet
› Handplane
› Power planer
› Bandsaw
› Router with ½-in. double flute straight bit
› Straightedge
› Tablesaw
› Random orbit sander
› Double-sided adhesive
› Carrier board
› Glue
› Food-safe finish

MATERIALS

› 1 live-edge slab of your choice, size will vary
› 2 pieces of walnut 1-in. wide and cut to the width of your slab

The board I used for this design came from a walnut tree at my childhood home in northwest Ohio. My stepfather cut the slab with a chainsaw, and the wood itself has a beautiful rustic look I love. I love the way the heartwood transitions to sapwood. And while I removed the bark so that it wouldn't flake off or collect bacteria over time, I retained the look of a live edge.

PLAN

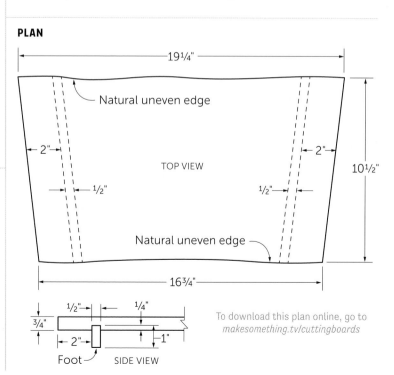

To download this plan online, go to *makesomething.tv/cuttingboards*

— 1 —

Start with a slab.
This 11"-wide walnut slab was rough cut with a chainsaw (and from a tree cut down at my childhood home—it has been air drying for a few years). Remove all the bark using a chisel and mallet but leave the natural, curvy edge of the sapwood.

— 2 —

Begin the flattening process.
Because this slab is twisted to the point where it won't sit flat on the planer bed, I take down the high spots with a handplane until the wobble has been removed. This may or may not be necessary with your slab.

— 3 —
You may need a carrier board.
If your slab needed a few passes with a handplane to take down the high spots, apply double-sided adhesive over the areas that were planed. Then attach the slab to a carrier board that will allow it to run through the planer.

— 4 —
Plane it to thickness.
Run the slab through the planer. Once the top side is flat, the slab can be removed from the carrier board. Once the top is smooth, flip the board over and flatten the bottom side.

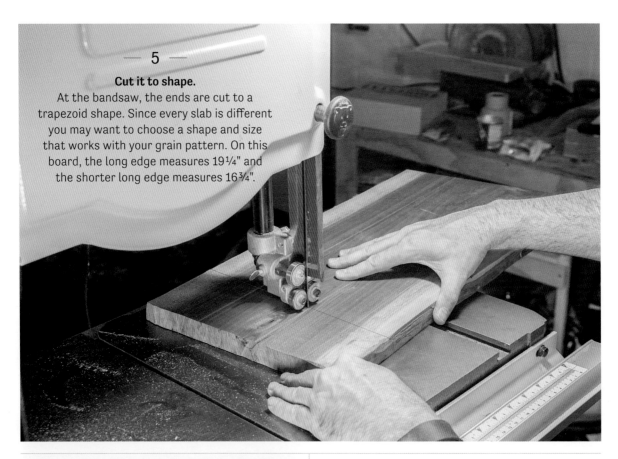

— 5 —

Cut it to shape.
At the bandsaw, the ends are cut to a trapezoid shape. Since every slab is different you may want to choose a shape and size that works with your grain pattern. On this board, the long edge measures 19¼" and the shorter long edge measures 16¾".

— 6 —

Ready the router.
To cut a groove that will house the feet on the cutting board, install a ½" double flute straight bit in your handheld router.

— 7 —

Rout out for the feet.
Draw in the dado for the feet about 2" in
from the ends of the board. Then position
a straightedge so that when the router
base is butted against it, the bit cuts in the
desired location. Then rout a ¼" deep dado
on each side parallel to the edges.

— 8 —

Cut out the feet.
To create the feet, use your tablesaw to
rip two strips of walnut to 1" wide.

— 9 —

Plane it to fit.
Run the two lengths of feet through the
planer. Remove stock in small increments
until the stock fits snugly in the dadoes on
the underside of the cutting board.

— 10 —

Trim them to length.
Slide the stock for the feet into the dadoes
on the cutting board and mark out their
length. At the bandsaw or using a handsaw,
cut them to length.

— 11 —

Attach the feet.
Apply a bead of glue in the dadoes and then
press the feet into place. If the fit is snug,
use a mallet to make sure they're fully
seated in the dadoes. If you have a nice
snug fit, clamps are unnecessary.

— 12 —

Sand it smooth.

Sand both the faces and edges of the cutting board smooth, working your way up to at least 220-grit sandpaper. On the edges, make sure all the soft bark has been sanded away to reveal the lighter sapwood.

— 13 —

Finish it off.

Apply a few coats of your food-safe finish of choice. For a detailed explanation on finishing cutting boards, see page 156.

CUTTING BOARD
SUSHI

Small, light, and elegant with a subtle Eastern flair

TOOLS & SUPPLIES

› Tablesaw with crosscut sled or miter gauge
› Permanent marker
› Combination square
› Wrench socket or other round object for foot profile
› Bandsaw
› Spindle sander
› Sanding blocks
› Clamps
› Disc sander
› Random orbit sander
› Double-sided tape
› Glue
› Food-safe finish

MATERIALS

› 5 pieces of hard maple ¾ x ¾ x 15-in.
› 2 pieces of walnut 1¾ x 1 x 15-in.

The walnut stripes not only contrast nicely with the maple, but also present a refined way of adding feet. Because the design has an Eastern feel, I refer to this design as a sushi board—and it does a heroic job of serving it up—but it also works great as a cheese plate or any time small cutting or serving tasks arise.

PLAN

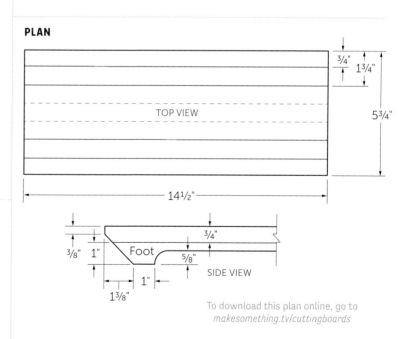

To download this plan online, go to
makesomething.tv/cuttingboards

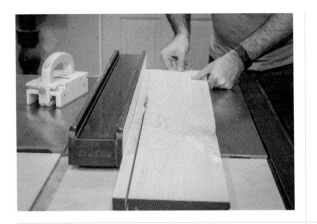

— 1 —
Prepare the maple.
Begin by cutting hard maple into square strips measuring ¾" x ¾".

— 2 —
Crosscut it to length.
Use a crosscut sled or miter gauge on your tablesaw to cut the hard maple strips to 15" long. You'll need a total of five pieces.

— 3 —
Prepare the walnut feet.
To act as both the feet and accent strips down the cutting board, cut two pieces of walnut to 15" long.

— 4 —
Trim them to size.
Rip the two pieces of walnut
to width at 1¾".

— 5 —
Draw out the feet.
Draw out the profile of the two feet on the
walnut stock. The ends have a 45° angle and
I use a wrench socket to draw my curves
on the underside.

— 6 —
Cut two feet at one time.
Cut out the foot pattern on the bandsaw. As
shown here, you can use double-sided tape
to stick the two pieces together and cut
them out at the same time.

— 7 —

Sand the feet.
While still taped together, use a spindle and sanding blocks to sand the legs to 220 grit.

— 8 —

Glue it up.
Spread a thin layer of glue between mating faces and bring the whole assembly together with clamps. You should have three pieces of maple between the walnut feet and one on each end.

— 9 —

Bevel the ends.
Next you'll create the beveled ends. This can be done using a disc sander or on a tablesaw outfitted with a miter gauge.

— 10 —

Make it smooth.
Use a random orbit sander to smooth
the face and edge of the cutting board.
Progress through finer and finer grits
until you reach 220.

— 11 —

Finish it off.
Apply your favorite food-safe finish.
For more on choosing and using
cutting boards, see page 156.

To see a video of this design being built, go to *makesomething.tv*.

PIZZA PEEL

A handmade peel for a handmade pie

TOOLS & SUPPLIES

- › Miter saw
- › Clamps
- › Large compass or pizza pan to trace
- › Pencil
- › Spray paint can for tracing handle
- › Bandsaw
- › Disc sander
- › Spindle sander
- › Rotary tool or rasp and file
- › Belt sander
- › Router table with ¾-in. roundover bit
- › Drill press with 1-in. bit
- › Random orbit sander
- › Glue
- › Food-safe finish

MATERIALS

- › 2 outside pieces: hickory ½ x 4½ x 15-in.
- › 1 center piece: mahogany ½ x 3¾ x 30-in.
- › 1 handle: mahogany ¾ x 3¾ x 15-in. (handle)

Homemade pizza is a mainstay at my house, but I never knew how much I needed a pizza peel until I made one. It's great for getting pies in and out of the oven and comes in handy for slicing and serving as well. When not in use, it's as handsome hanging on your kitchen wall as it is useful on pizza night.

PLAN

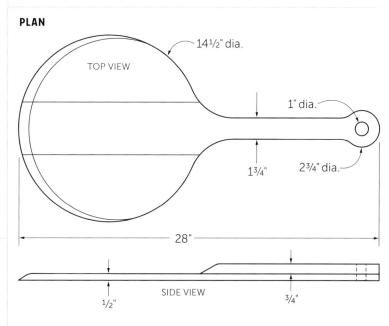

To download this plan online, go to
makesomething.tv/cuttingboards

— 1 —

Buy or plane your stock.
You can plane thicker stock down to ½",
or buy pre-thickenessed ½"-thick stock
from your local hardwood dealer.

— 2 —

Survey your stock.
The combination of mahogany and
hickory lend a nice look to this design, but
any contrasting, food-safe hardwoods
would work as well.

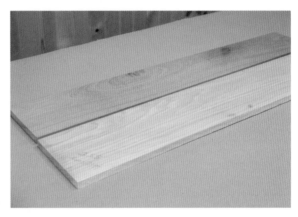

— 3 —

Rough out the stock.
Begin by crosscutting the two
outside pieces (hickory) to roughly
15" long and the single middle piece
(mahogany) to roughly 30".

— 4 —

Glue it up.
Clamp and glue everything together, trying to keep all the pieces level and aligned. Spring clamps positioned at the joint lines help keep the pieces aligned.

— 5 —

Draw out a circle.
You can use a large compass or outline the profile of a round pan. Shown here is a 14½" pizza pan.

— 6 —

Draw out the handle.
The straight portion of the handle is
1¾" wide. To create the curved transition
from the handle to the rounded portion of
the board, you can draw the curve freehand
or trace the pattern off a can, jar,
or large washer.

— 7 —

Round the end.
At the end of the handle, draw out
another circle—tracing the base of a spray
paint can works perfectly. Again, blend the
transition from the circle into the handle
lines. The total length of the pizza peel
should be about 28".

— 8 —

Cut the peel to shape.

Cut out the shape of the peel at the bandsaw. Trim as close to the line as possible, making sure you don't actually cut into or over the line. In later steps you can refine and finalize the shape.

— 9 —

Clean up the edges.

Use a disc sander to sand down to the layout lines on the convex edges of the peel.

— 10 —

Smooth the handle.

A spindle sander does a good job of fairing and smoothing the tight inside corners on the handle.

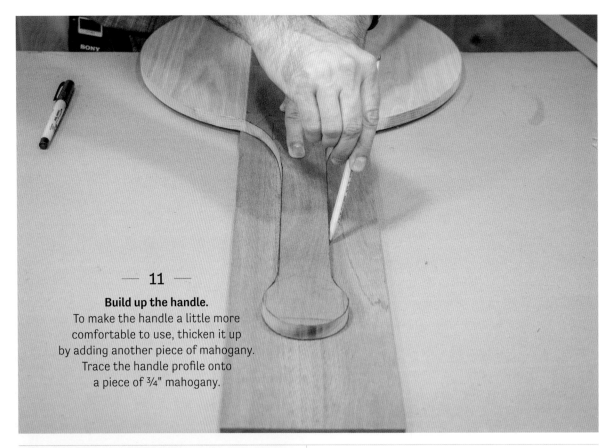

— 11 —

Build up the handle.
To make the handle a little more comfortable to use, thicken it up by adding another piece of mahogany. Trace the handle profile onto a piece of ¾" mahogany.

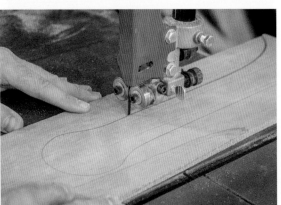

— 12 —

Cut to the line.
Cut out the handle shape at the bandsaw. Again, cut as close as possible to the line without touching it.

— 13 —
Create a transition.
Where the handle meets the large round end of the peel, draw a curve that will blend into the main part of the pizza peel.

— 14 —
Cut out the waste.
Back at the bandsaw, cut to the line to remove the waste from the transition area on the handle addition.

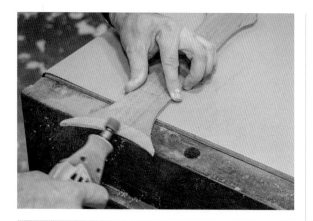

— 15 —
Cut a smooth transition.
Create a bevel onto the additional handle stock so that it will blend into the large end of the peel. A rotary tool works well to remove the wood, but a rasp and file would work as well.

— 16 —
Clamp it up.
Glue and clamp the new handle material to the main handle of the peel.

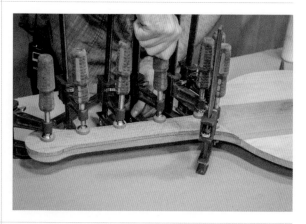

— 17 —
Smooth it out.
Once the glue dries, sand everything flush at the spindle sander or with a file and sandpaper.

— 18 —
Draw out the bevel.
A bevel on the front edge of a peel allows it to slide under a pizza easily. You can draw out the guidelines for the bevel freehand. Draw the line in from the edge about 1" at the end and taper it down so that it's flush at the sides of the peel.

— 19 —
Shape the bevel.
File or sand away the wood to create a nice wedge shape on the front of the peel. This can be done quickly with a belt sander and 80-grit sandpaper.

— 20 —

Round the handle edges.
Use a ¾" roundover bit in your router
table to soften the edges of the handle.
You only need to round over the top face
of the handle. The bottom of the handle
and the pizza area will have a much smaller
roundover, which can be shaped by hand.

— 21 —

Drill it out.
Centered on the round end of the handle,
drill a 1" hole so you can hang up your
peel for storage and display.

— 22 —

Sand it smooth.
Sand the faces up to 220 grit using a
random orbit sander. Be sure to blend all
the curves and round over any sharp edges.

— 23 —
Finish it off.
This board was finished using a heavy coat
of food-grade mineral oil and paraffin wax,
but any food-safe finish would work.
For more details on finishing, see page 156.

— 24 —
Have a slice!
All that's left to do is bake a pizza
and put your pizza peel to use.

SCRAP WOOD

Make the most of your leftovers

TOOLS & SUPPLIES

› Miter saw or tablesaw with miter gauge
› Clamps
› Power planer
› Drum sander or random orbit sander
› Router with 45° chamfer bit or roundover bit
› Glue
› Food-safe finish
› 4 rubber feet with stainless steel screws

MATERIALS

› Scrap wood in various widths, 1½-in. thick x 20-in. long

If I ever walk into a shop that doesn't have at least one stack of scrap wood in the corner, I'll know it's a front for something nefarious. This is the perfect time to shorten your own scrap stack. This end grain design stands up well to knives and is practically self-healing when cut. And if you're going to make one, make many—these designs are perfect for building in batches to give as gifts.

PLAN

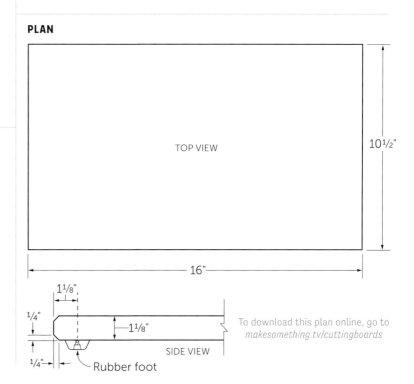

TOP VIEW

10½"

16"

1⅛"

¼"

1⅛"

¼"

SIDE VIEW

Rubber foot

To download this plan online, go to
makesomething.tv/cuttingboards

— 1 —
Clean up the shop.
It's finally time to put that that bucket (or box, or closet, or shed) of scrap wood you've been collecting to use. Gather a collection of boards that vary in color and grain pattern. The boards seen here are enough to make two different cutting boards. Cutting enough stock for multiple boards gives you more options for laying out the random design.

— 2 —
Cut the stock to length.
Begin by cutting all your scrap pieces to 20" in length at either the miter saw or using a tablesaw outfitted with a miter gauge.

— 3 —
Rip it to width.
At the tablesaw, rip all those pieces to a uniform width of 1½". To help keep the stock flush to the blade and your hands far away from it, use a push stick.

— 4 —

Lay out your design.
Arrange your wood into a random pattern, alternating boards for contrast and whim. Shown here are patterns for two cutting boards.

— 5 —

Glue it up.
Lay a thin layer of glue onto mating faces and then bring it all together using clamps to secure everything in place.

— 6 —

Plane it down.
Once the glue dries, run the entire
assembly through the thickness planer.
Be sure to take passes on both faces
to ensure that both are smooth and
that the thickness is uniform.

— 7 —

Crosscut the panel.
At the tablesaw, use a crosscut sled
or miter gauge to cut the assembled panel
into 1¼" strips. Feel free to make your
crosscuts wider if you want to make
a thicker cutting board.

8

Reassemble the boards.
You can now glue everything back together, being sure that the end grain is faceup and the pattern is random. If you're making two boards, you can swap out pieces from each to increase the randomness.

9

Sand everything flush.
Because a thickness planer doesn't handle end grain very well, sand both faces of the cutting board until they are both flush and smooth. A drum sander makes it a quick job, but a random orbit sander will work as well.

— 10 —
Square it up.
At the tablesaw, you can both square up the assembly and clean up any glue squeeze-out on the edges of the board.

— 11 —
Soften the hard edges.
Outfit your router with a 45° chamfer bit to cut and remove the sharp edges on both the top and bottom. If you prefer rounded edges, choose a roundover bit instead.

— 12 —
Smooth it out.
Sand both the faces and edges of the cutting boards, progressing through finer and finer grits up to 220.

— 13 —

Finish it off.
Wipe on your favorite food-safe finish.
This board is finished with a mix of wax and
mineral oil, but feel free to apply your
food-safe finish of choice. For more
on finishing options and techniques,
check out page 156.

— 14 —

Add rubber feet.
Simple rubber feet raise the cutting board
off your countertop and add grip to help it
stay in place while you work. Be sure to use
stainless steel screws to prevent rust.

OVER THE PLATE

This clever and resilient design is a kitchen workhorse

TOOLS & SUPPLIES

› Sliding compound miter saw or tablesaw with crosscut sled or miter gauge
› Ruler
› Pencil
› Bandsaw
› Can of spray paint or other round object to trace corners
› 11-in. dinner plate
› Disc sander
› Spindle sander
› Glue
› Food-safe finish
› 4 rubber feet with stainless steel screws

MATERIALS

› Cutting board: 1 piece of bamboo plywood, ¾ x 12 x 19-in.
› Feet: 4 pieces of bamboo plywood, ¾ x 3 x 3-in.

I love making kitchenware out of bamboo. It stands up well to water and weathers knife cuts with little visible wear. And because it comes in sheet form, it's easy to work with in the shop. This design is straight-forward, but endlessly handy in the kitchen. The board itself is elevated; one edge is shaped so you can slide off cuts onto a dinner plate that fits easily underneath the lip of the board.

PLAN

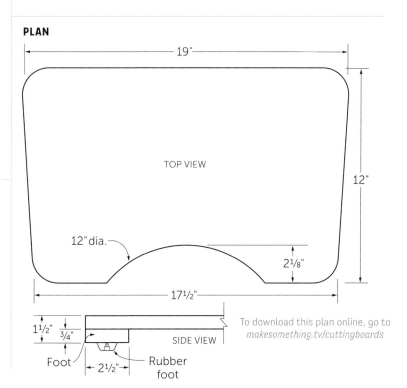

To download this plan online, go to *makesomething.tv/cuttingboards*

— 1 —

Cut the stock to size.
Start with a 12"-wide piece of
¾"-thick bamboo and cut it to length at 19".
Use either a sliding compound miter saw
or a tablesaw outfitted with a
crosscut sled or miter gauge.

— 2 —

Mark out the trapezoid.
Measure ¾" in from each of
the two bottom edges and make
a tick mark at each point.

— 3 —

Draw in the two ends.
Using a straightedge as your guide, draw
a pencil line from the pencil marks you just
made to their adjacent corners.

— 4 —

Cut out the tapers.
At the bandsaw, follow your two lines to remove the stock on the ends. You could make this same cut using a tablesaw outfitted with a miter gauge.

— 5 —

Mark out rounded corners.
Use the edge of a can of finish or spray paint as a guide to draw out your radiuses on each corner.

— 6 —

Round the corners.
At the bandsaw, remove the waste by
cutting to the line on all four corners.

— 7 —

Position the plate.
Centered along the short edge of the board,
mark out the profile of an 11" dinner plate.

— 8 —

Adjust the arch.
Since the dinner plate will slide further back into the board, freehand a curved line that is slightly larger than the original tracing.

— 9 —

Create the cutout.
Back at the bandsaw, cut to the larger curve you drew in freehand.

— 10 —

Draw out the feet.
To create the feet of the cutting board,
trace out four circles using the same can
you used to draw out the rounded corners.

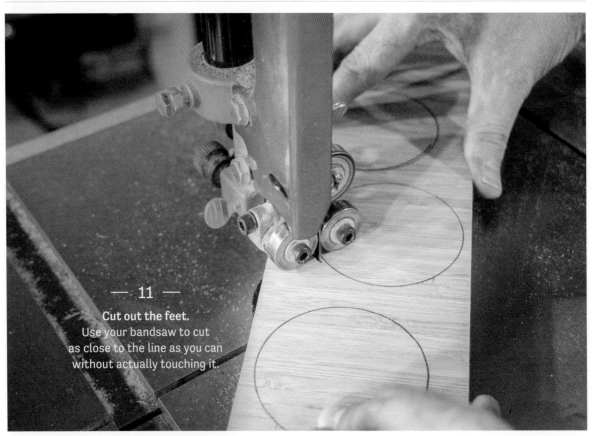

— 11 —

Cut out the feet.
Use your bandsaw to cut
as close to the line as you can
without actually touching it.

— 12 —
Round them off.
Sand down to the line to shape and smooth the edges of all four feet using a disc sander.

— 13 —
Attach the feet.
Glue and clamp the feet to the bottom of the cutting board. Try to flush up the edges of the feet to the edges of the cutting board, keeping in mind that you'll then finalize the shape in the next step.

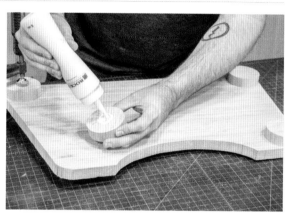

— 14 —
Flush up the edges.
Use a disc sander or a sanding block to smooth the straight edges and flush the feet to the rounded corners.

— 15 —

Smooth the curved edge.
A spindle sander works well to smooth and fair the edge of the cutting board that is curved to accommodate the plate. Alternately, use a length of sandpaper wrapped around a large dowel.

— 16 —

The final sanding.
Sand the faces of both the top and bottom to 220 grit using a random orbit sander.

— 17 —

Rub on a finish.
This board is finished with a combination of mineral oil and wax, but you can use your food-safe finish of choice. For more on food-safe finishing options, see page 156.

— 18 —

Give it some grip.
Once the finish dries, install rubber feet on the bottom of the cutting board. The rubber feet help stabilize the board and give it enough lift to allow a plate to slide underneath. Be sure to use stainless steel screws to prevent rust.

OVER THE SINK

A design that does double-duty

TOOLS & SUPPLIES

> Tablesaw
> Clamps
> Power planer
> Pencil
> Drill
> Jigsaw with wood cutting blade
> Spindle sander or sandpaper wrapped around a dowel
> Router with ¼-in. rabbeting bit and ¼-in. roundover bit
> Can of finish or other round object to trace corners
> Bandsaw or jigsaw
> Random orbit sander
> Glue
> 7½-in. (or size of choice) mesh stainless steel colander
> Food-safe finish

With this cutting board, you can not only cut your veggies, you can also wash them in the sink. It is a custom but straightforward design that can be made in only a few hours. Just be sure to buy your strainer before you make the cutout, and alter the overall size to fit your particular sink.

MATERIALS

> Outer edges: 2 pieces of red oak, ¾ x 4 x 18½-in. (width may vary to fit your particular sink)
> Thin accents: 2 pieces of bubinga, ¾ x ⅜ x 18½-in.
> Main pieces: 2 pieces of red oak, ¾ x ⅜ x 18½-in.
> Center accent: 1 piece of bubinga, ¾ x 1¼ x 18½-in.

PLAN

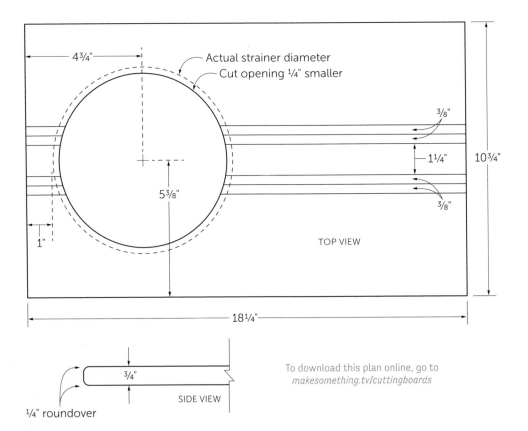

Actual strainer diameter
Cut opening ¼" smaller

4¾"

3/8"

1¼"

10¾"

3/8"

5⅜"

1"

TOP VIEW

18¼"

¾"

SIDE VIEW

¼" roundover

To download this plan online, go to
makesomething.tv/cuttingboards

— 1 —

Cut the stock to length.
This cutting board will be made up of mostly
red oak. I'm using ¾"-thick stock from the
home center. Cut it to length at 18½".

— 2 —

Cut an accent wood.
Bubinga, shown here, contrasts well with the red oak, but walnut or other dark woods would work as well. Cut the contrasting wood to length at 18½".

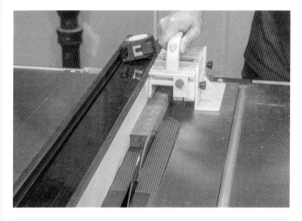

— 3 —

Create the middle strip.
At the tablesaw, rip the accent wood to 1¼" wide. When making thin cuts, a push stick helps keep your hands clear of the blade.

— 4 —

Break down the red oak.
Cut the two outer edge pieces of the red oak to 4" wide. Feel free to adjust this measurement to work with the dimensions of your sink.

— 5 —

Create oak accents.
Two thin strips of oak are used
to make up the accent strips.
Rip the inner accent pieces to ⅜" wide.

— 6 —

Cut thin strips of accent wood.
With the rip fence still set to ⅜" wide,
rip two lengths of the accent wood.

— 7 —

Lay it out.
You should now have seven pieces
ready for glue-up:
Outer red oak — 4" x 18½" (x 2)
Inner red oak accents — ⅜" x 18½" (x 2)
Bubinga accents — ⅜" x 18½" (x 2)
Bubinga center — 1¼" x 18½" (x 1)

— 8 —
Glue it up.
Glue and clamp everything together using a water-resistant yellow wood glue. You can tweak it later, but aim to keep everything aligned both in thickness and length.

— 9 —
Plane it smooth.
Once the glue dries, run the assembly through the planer to flatten it. Keep the board as thick as possible because thinner cutting boards often warp over time as they get wet.

— 10 —
Trim it to length.
Use a miter gauge to square up one end of the cutting board. Then cut the other end square and to a final length of 18¼".

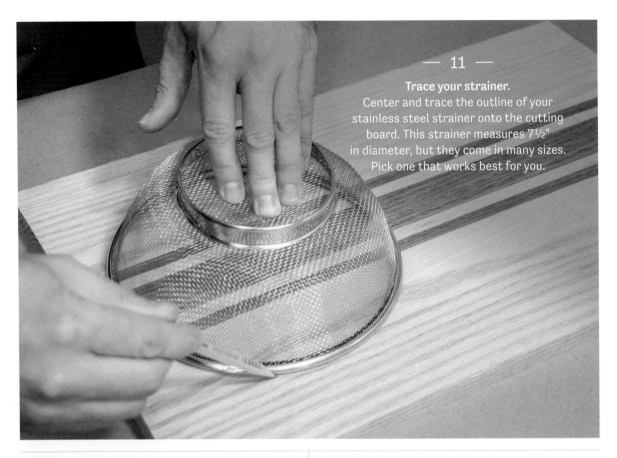

— 11 —

Trace your strainer.

Center and trace the outline of your stainless steel strainer onto the cutting board. This strainer measures 7½" in diameter, but they come in many sizes. Pick one that works best for you.

— 12 —

Mark an inner line.

Draw a circle ¼" inside the outline of the strainer. Cutting to this line will prevent the strainer from falling through the cutting board.

— 13 —
Start with a drilled hole.
Drill a ½" hole—or any diameter that is larger enough to accomodate your jigsaw blade — within the inner circle on your cutting board.

— 14 —
Cut it out.
Starting with your jigsaw in the drilled hole, cut out the inner circle, following the line as closely as you can.

— 15 —
Clean it up.
Smooth out rough cuts using a spindle sander or a length of sandpaper wrapped around a dowel.

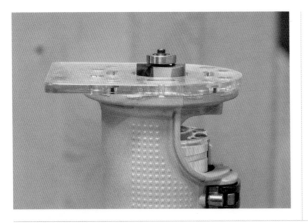

— 16 —
Ready the router.
Install a ¼" rabbeting bit in your router
and set it to cut ¼" deep.

— 17 —
Rout it out.
Working clockwise, cut a rabbet around
the top of the circle. This creates a lip
for the strainer to rest on but still sit
below the surface of the cutting board.

— 18 —

Round it off.
Use a can of finish or other
round object and trace the profile
onto the corners of the board.

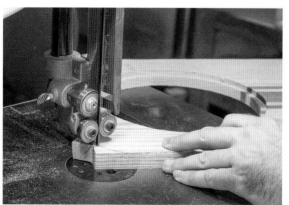

— 19 —

Make the cuts.
Use a bandsaw or jigsaw to
trim away the waste on the
four corners of the cutting board.

— 20 —

Clean up the edges.
A disc sander makes for easy cleanup of the rounded corners, but a sheet of sandpaper wrapped around a sanding block will work as well.

— 21 —

Round over the edges.
Install a ¼" roundover bit in your router and round the outer edges of the cutting board. This can be done with a handheld router or at the router table, as shown here.

— 22 —

Smooth it out.
Sand everything smooth up to 220 grit
using a random orbit sander or by hand.

— 23 —

Finish it off.
A few coats of mineral oil and wax
make a nice food-safe finish. For a
detailed explanation on finishing
cutting boards see page 156.

RAMEKINS

Mise-en-place for easy ingredient sorting

TOOLS & SUPPLIES

› Tablesaw
› Sliding compound miter saw
› Clamps
› Compass
› Ruler
› Drill
› Screws
› Drill press
› 3½-in. hole saw
› ¾-in. diameter drill bit
› Spindle sander or sandpaper wrapped around a dowel
› Bandsaw
› Random orbit sander
› Glue
› 4 ramekins
› Food-safe finish
› 4 rubber feet with stainless steel screws

MATERIALS

› Main board: 2 pieces of bamboo plywood, ¾ x 12 x 18-in.
› Accent layer: 2 pieces of mahogany, ¼ x 12 x 18-in.

The inclusion of four ramekins in this board makes it perfect for separating ingredients into dishes as you chop them. Built from bamboo plywood, it's also hefty and will last for years. Make sure to size the holes to fit your particular ramekins.

PLAN

1" radius

TOP VIEW

1¼"

½"   ½"   ½"

1¼"

12"

3½" dia.

¾" dia.

½"

18"

1⅛"

¼"

Ramekin hole 1¾" deep

¾"

¾"

SIDE VIEW

Rubber foot

To download this plan online, go to
makesomething.tv/cuttingboards

— 1 —

Cut the bamboo to size.
Begin by ripping the bamboo plywood to 12" wide at the tablesaw. Then cut two pieces of bamboo to length. You can use either a sliding compound miter saw or a crosscut sled on your tablesaw.

— 2 —

Prepare the accents.
The caramel tones of mahogany compliment the warm tones of the bamboo. To create the accent pieces, cut a ¼"-thick piece of mahogany to 18" long.

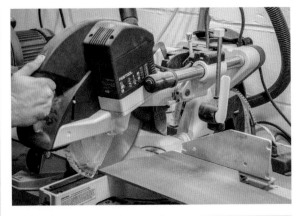

— 3 —

Create the center panel.
Plane enough mahogany stock to create an 12"-wide panel that is ¼" thick. Then edge-glue and clamp the mahogany stock.

— 4 —

Draw out the ramekin locations. Measure the diameter of your ramekins, then use a compass to draw out their positions on one of the bamboo panels. When positioning the centerpoints of the ramekin locations, measure down 2¼" from the top edge of the cutting board, as shown in the drawing on page 65.

— 5 —

Drill the finger holes.
Before drilling the ramekin holes, drill the finger holes in the top layer of bamboo. The center of these ¾" holes is positioned on the bigger circles 1" down from the top.

— 6 —

Secure the layers in place.
Clamp the two pieces of bamboo and the mahogany accent piece in place, but do not apply glue. Drive screws into the four corners to hold everything in place.

— 7 —

Cut some large holes.
Install a 3½" hole saw bit in your drill press and bore holes at the four center points marked on the cutting board. When boring, pause between each layer to remove the waste from the bit.

— 8 —

Smooth them out.
Once the holes are drilled, use a spindle sander (or a length of sandpaper wrapped around a dowel) to smooth the edges.

— 9 —

Glue up the layers.
Remove the four screws used as temporary clamps and lay a thin coat of glue onto each layer. Screw them back together using the same screw holes to align them perfectly. Add clamps and allow it to dry for a few hours.

— 10 —
Create the lower panel.
For the bottom layer of the cutting board assembly, glue up another panel that measures 18" x 12".

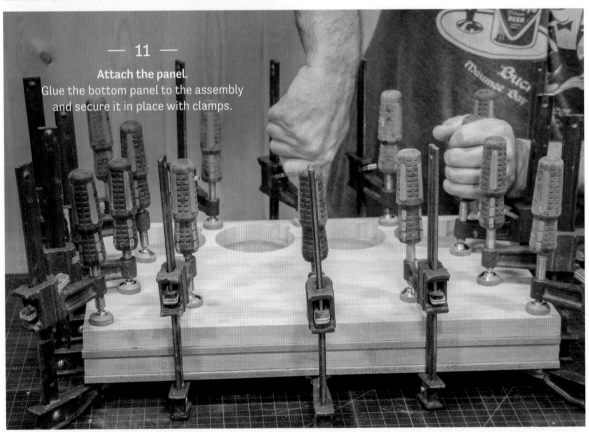

— 11 —
Attach the panel.
Glue the bottom panel to the assembly and secure it in place with clamps.

— 12 —

Clean it up.
Sand or cut all four edges
to create crisp edges
all the way around.

— 13 —

Draw out the corners.
Using one of the ramekins as a template,
draw the rounded corners.

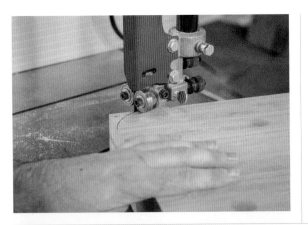

— 14 —

Shape the corners.
Use your bandsaw to cut away excess on
the four corners of the board.

— 15 —

Smooth it out.
A random orbit sander makes quick
work of smoothing out both the edges
and faces of the cutting board.
Progress through finer and finer grits
until you reach 220.

— 16 —
Lay on the finish.
For this board I use a combination of mineral oil and wax, but any food-safe finish will work. For more information on finishing cutting boards, check out page 156.

— 17 —
Give it a lift.
Apply rubber feet to the bottom of the cutting board at all four corners. Be sure to use stainless steel screws to prevent rust.

CHEESEBOARD & KNIFE

A rustic, one-of-a-kind set from salvaged lumber

TOOLS & SUPPLIES

› Sliding compound miter saw
› Drill press
› 1½-in. drill bit
› Pencil
› Bandsaw
› Chisel
› Two-part epoxy
› Food-safe finish

MATERIALS

› Cheeseboard:
  1 live-edge board, roughly,
  ¾ x 7½ x 17½-in.
› Knife: 1 hardwood scrap,
  ⅜ x ⅞ x 6¼-in.

The 100-year-old barn plank I used to make this cheeseboard and spreader is one of those small but unique boards that tells a story. My aim was to highlight the age and patina of the wood itself; leaving the live edge helps. The board is simple, but a handmade spreader made from the same board makes it a beautiful and one-of-a-kind set that begs to be touched. Just remember, when using rustic or rough lumber, cover any holes or crevices to prevent bacteria from hiding.

PLAN

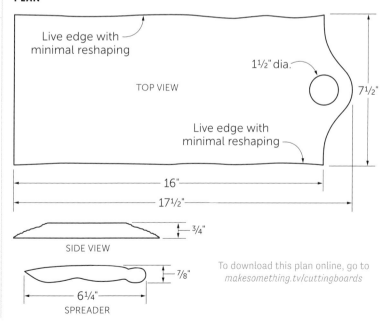

Live edge with minimal reshaping

1½" dia.

TOP VIEW

7½"

Live edge with minimal reshaping

16"

17½"

¾"

SIDE VIEW

⅞"

6¼"

SPREADER

To download this plan online, go to
makesomething.tv/cuttingboards

— 1 —

Find the right board.
To create a cheeseboard and knife with style, choose stock with character, like this live-edge length of air-dried oak barn siding. Because it was cut from near the bark of the tree, the bottom edge is curved like the outside of the tree.

— 2 —

Cut it to length.
The overall width of this cheeseboard is 7½". Before cutting it to length with a miter saw, be sure the wavy edge of the board is secure against the saw fence.

— 3 —

Drill it out.
In one end of the board drill a 1½" hole, which serves both as a handle for use when serving and a convenient way to hang the board for storage or display.

— 4 —
Freehand the shape.
Because it's a live-edge board, there's no reason to keep everything square or symmetrical. Simple curves around the hole in the handle can be drawn in freehand.

— 5 —
Cut it out.
Use your bandsaw to cut to the line drawn onto the end of the board. Be sure to place the flat side of the board flat on your bandsaw table to ensure that it remains stable throughout the cut.

— 6 —

Form a bevel on the end.
To mirror the upward sweep on the sides of the board, use a chisel to carve a roughly ¼" bevel on the shaped end.

— 7 —

Fill in any imperfections.
Because I'm using rustic wood with imperfections, I'm filling the holes with epoxy. Dip a pencil in epoxy and drip it into the holes. These holes need to be filled in to prevent bacteria from growing in them.

— 8 —

Stabilize the edge.
The waney edge of the wood is liable
to flake off after use and over time.
To stabilize the edge, brush on a coat
of two-part epoxy.

— 9 —

Draw out the knife.
On a small scrap of wood, draw
out the profile of your knife
freehand. Use a simple dinner
knife as a rough guide or simply
draw out your own from scratch.

— 10 —

Cut the profile.
At the bandsaw, cut out the profile of the knife. The knife doesn't have to fit any specific shape, but follow the line as best you can. Because this is a small workpiece, take extra care to make sure fingers steer clear of the blade.

— 11 —

Rip it to width.
Turn the knife onto the back of its handle and rip it down to width. Aim for a comfortable width at the handle and taper down to a finer "knife" end.

— 12 —
Sand it smooth.
Use a random orbit sander or sandpaper to get the knife to its final shape. Here, there are two knives because I'm making two cheeseboard sets. This is an easy project to make a few of at once.

— 13 —
Lay on the finish.
This board is finished using a combination of food-grade mineral oil and wax, but you can use your finish of choice. For more on food-safe finishing options, see page 156.

END GRAIN

A cutting board built for the long haul

TOOLS & SUPPLIES

› Power planer
› Tablesaw with crosscut sled or miter gauge
› Clamps
› Router table with ¾-in. roundover bit and cove bit
› Random orbit sander
› Glue
› Food-safe finish
› 4 rubber feet with stainless steel screws

MATERIALS

› 1 piece of maple, 2 x 7½ x 20-in.
› 1 piece of walnut, 2 x 6 x 20-in.

End grain cutting boards are built to stand up to heavy use for years. They're self-healing and seldom show knife marks. They're also easier on knife edges, which reduces sharpening time. There are numerous patterns you can create with the grain on the blocks. I also like the contrast of having a light maple center surrounded by a band of walnut blocks.

PLAN

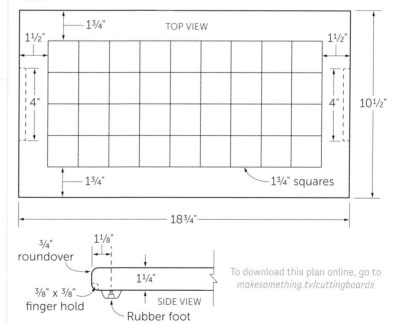

To download this plan online, go to *makesomething.tv/cuttingboards*

— 1 —
Thickness your stock.
To make an end grain cutting board, starting with stock that is all uniform in thickness is critical. When in doubt, cut a little extra stock — it's difficult to go back and mill stock to the exact same thickness later.

— 2 —
Do so all at once.
Take alternating passes between the maple and walnut stock, incrementally lowering the cutterhead only after you've run both boards through at each thickness level.

— 3 —
Rip it to width.
Set the fence to cut stock that matches the thickness of the stock, then rip all of your boards to width.

— 4 —
Prepare the contrasting stock.
Before adjusting the setting on your tablesaw fence, be sure to rip all of the walnut as well.

— 5 —
Crosscut to length.
Using a tablesaw outfitted with a crosscut sled or miter gauge, cut all of the maple stock to 20" lengths.

— 6 —
Glue up the maple.
Lay a thin layer of glue onto mating edges and then clamp four lengths of maple together.

— 7 —

Prepare the walnut.

Cut the lengths of walnut to short lengths of 1¼". To guarantee uniform thickness, set a stop on your crosscut sled or miter gauge. Just be sure to remove the stop before making each cut.

— 8 —

Glue it up.

Glue and clamp four sections of walnut to make up the perimeter of the cutting board — two ends and two sides. To make assembly less stressful, you may build up each length in multiple glue-ups. In the end, you should have two that are 12 blocks long and two that are 5 blocks long.

— 9 —

Thickness the slab.

Run the assembled maple slab through the thickness planer, making sure both sides are smooth and that the entire assembly is of uniform thickness.

— 10 —
Cut it up.
Crosscut the maple slab across its width using the same stop distance you used for cutting the walnut blocks.

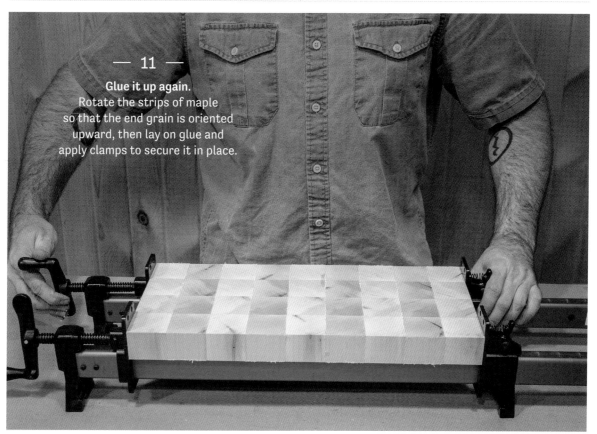

— 11 —
Glue it up again.
Rotate the strips of maple so that the end grain is oriented upward, then lay on glue and apply clamps to secure it in place.

— 12 —

Clean up the edges.

To clean up any glue squeeze-out and to create a smooth, straight edge, crosscut the ends and sides of the maple assembly.

— 13 —

Add the end.

Line up the gluelines between the walnut ends and the maple center. Then lay on the glue and clamp it up again.

— 14 —

Clean up the edges.

Removing as little material as possible, rip a tiny sliver off the long edges of the assembly. This will clean up any glue squeeze-out and leave a nice crisp edge for glue-up.

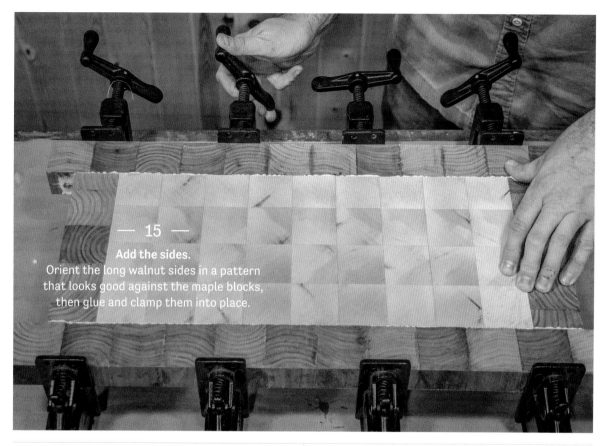

— 15 —

Add the sides.
Orient the long walnut sides in a pattern
that looks good against the maple blocks,
then glue and clamp them into place.

— 16 —

Trim off the waste.
Crosscut the ends of the cutting board to
leave a square, clean edge.

— 17 —

Soften the edges.
Use a ¾" roundover bit at the router table to round the edges of both the top and bottom of the cutting board.

— 18 —

Cut out a handle.
Using a cove bit in your router table, set up two stops on the fence and plunge cut to create centered fingerholds on the ends of the board.

— 19 —

Sand it smooth.
Sanding end grain takes a little more time and patience than sanding face grain, but it's time well spent. Start at a coarser grit than usual — maybe 120 — and progress through grits to 220 or higher.

— 20 —

Finish it off.
Use a lint-free cotton rag to lay on
your favorite food-safe finish.
For more on choosing and using
finishes for cutting boards, see page 156.

— 21 —

Screw on the feet.
Rubber feet on the bottom of the
board help it stay in place when in use.
Attach them using stainless steel
screws to prevent rust.

BREADBOARD ENDS

Use table-making techniques to create a beautiful cutting board

TOOLS & SUPPLIES

> Sliding compound miter saw
> Clamps
> Power planer
> Tablesaw with miter gauge
> Drill press
> Handheld drill
> ¼-in. drill bit
> Mallet or hammer
> Flush saw
> Chisel
> Glue
> Food-safe finish
> 4 rubber feet with stainless steel screws

MATERIALS

> Center: 1 piece of hickory: 2 x 12 x 18-in.
> Breadboard ends: 2 pieces of walnut, 2 x 2 x 12-in.
> Pegs: 1 hardwood dowel, ¼-in. diameter

Using breadboard ends is a classic technique for keeping stock flat while still allowing for wood movement. You could use the same skills to build a farmhouse-style dinner table. For this design, I chose walnut and hickory because I like the way the walnut helps highlight the dark tones in the hickory grain.

PLAN

To download this plan online, go to *makesomething.tv/cuttingboards*

— 1 —

Rough cut the stock.
Begin by cutting lengths of 8/4 (2" thick)
hickory stock to a length of 18". Cut enough
of the pieces to create a cutting board
12" wide when glued up edge-to-edge.

— 2 —

Create the panel.
Lay a thin layer of glue onto
mating edges and clamp them together
to create a single panel at full width.

— 3 —
Thickness the stock.
Run the panel through your thickness planer until the top of the panel is flat. Then flip the board over and flatten the underside as well. The exact overall thickness is less important than making sure the entire panel is of uniform thickness.

— 4 —
Prepare the breadboard ends.
Plane the stock you plan to use for breadboard ends down to the same thickness as the center panel.

— 5 —
Square it up.
At the tablesaw, use a miter gauge to square up the two ends of the center panel.

— 6 —

Cut the tongue.
Position the fence 1" from the blade and raise the blade to ⅜". Take multiple passes with a single blade to hog away the waste on the ends of the stock, with your last pass guided by the miter gauge but flush against the fence. Because you're removing the same amount from each face of the panel, the tongue is perfectly centered.

— 7 —

Raise the blade.
With the saw switched off, raise the blade until its height matches the depth of the tongue.

— 8 —

Cut the groove.
On the stock you're using for breadboard ends, take multiple passes to hog out the waste to accommodate the tongue. Be sure to take passes with both faces against the fence so that the tongue will be centered on the stock. Aim for a fit that is snug but goes together with only hand pressure.

— 9 —

Crosscut the breadboard ends.
Mark the width of the center panel directly onto the stock you're using for the breadboard ends. Use your tablesaw and miter gauge to crosscut it to length.

— 10 —

Rip it to width.
Now that all of the joinery has been cut, remove excess width on the breadboard ends by ripping them at the tablesaw.

— 11 —
Prepare for pegs.
Set the breadboard ends into position on the panel and drill three equally spaced holes on each end. The holes can go through both sides of the breadboard end as well as the tongue on the panel.

— 12 —
Allow wood to move.
The center holes on each end of the tongues can be left as they are and a peg will secure them in place. Use a hand drill or chisel to widen the four outer holes on the tongues. This extra room will allow the pegs to stay in the same spot on the breadboard ends as the main panel expands and contracts with humidity.

— 13 —

Glue it up.
To allow for inevitable wood movement, glue only the center 3" of the panel to the breadboard ends. The outer pegs will keep the ends flush against the shoulder on the panel even as the panel changes with humidity.

— 14 —

Install the pegs.
Clamp the breadboard ends to the panel tightly in place. Use a mallet or hammer to drive short lengths of ¼" dowel through the breadboard ends and tongue. Round over the leading edge of the pegs so they are easier to tap into place.
On the center dowels only, add a drop of glue before you sink the pegs.

— 15 —
Clean it up.
Use a flush cut saw to trim away
the ends of the pegs. If they're not quite
flush with the breadboard ends, use a
sharp chisel to clean up the cuts.

— 16 —
Cut the bevel.
Angle the blade on your tablesaw to
about 45°. Then bevel the lower edges
of the breadboard ends using a
miter gauge to guide your cut.

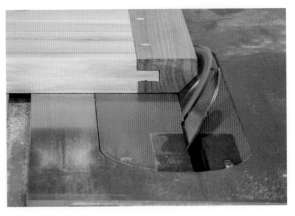

— 17 —
Seal up the imperfections.
Use a pencil dipped in epoxy to drip epoxy
into the knots so bacteria doesn't form
in the crevices.

— 18 —

Make it shine.
Use a lint-free cotton rag to wipe on your finish of choice. This board was finished with mineral oil and wax. For more on applying food-safe finishes, see page 156.

— 19 —

Give it a lift.
Screwing rubber feet onto the bottom of the cutting board at all four corners not only raises the cutting board up off your counter, it also lends a little grip so it is less likely to move when in use.

To see a video of this design being built, go to *makesomething.tv*.

ULU BOARD SET

A knife and board that are made for each other

MATERIALS

› Knife handle: 2 pieces of maple, ½ x 1½ x 3½-in.
› Outer edges of board: 2 pieces of maple, 1½ x 2½ x 8-in.
› Dark stripes: 2 pieces of walnut, 1½ x ¾ x 8-in.
› Center stripe: 1 piece of maple, 1½ x 1 x 8-in.

Years ago while visiting Alaska we picked up an ulu knife and the only thing I like better than how cool it looks is how well it works. The round blade and mating, scooped out cutting board make for efficient cutting of vegetables and herbs. This design is now our favorite and most-used knife and cutting board. Making the knife is a great introduction to basic metal work that doesn't require specialized tools. If you prefer to build the board but skip making the knife, you can buy one online or at any cooking store.

TOOLS & SUPPLIES

› Tablesaw
› Clamps
› Power planer
› Drill
› Screws
› Lathe
› Lathe tool: carbide tip rougher
› Self-healing cutting mat
› Craft knife
› Jigsaw with metal cutting blade
› Drill press
› Disc sander
› Belt sander
› Bastard file
› Random orbit sander
› Sandpaper
› Permanent marker
› Sharpening stones and oil or automotive sandpaper
› Bandsaw
› Hack saw or jigsaw
› Glue
› Food-safe finish
› Printed or drawn ulu knife pattern
› Spray adhesive
› 16 gauge stainless steel sheet metal
› 5-minute epoxy
› ¼-in. brass dowel rod

PLAN

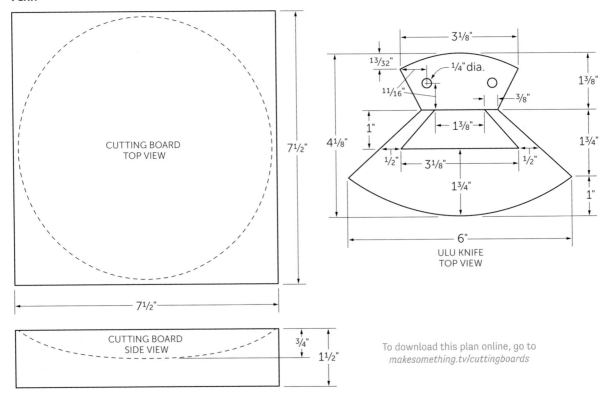

CUTTING BOARD
TOP VIEW

7½"

7½"

CUTTING BOARD
SIDE VIEW

¾"

1½"

3⅛"

¹³/₃₂"

¼" dia.

1⅜"

¹¹/₁₆"

⅜"

4⅛"

1"

1⅜"

1¾"

½"

3⅛"

½"

1¾"

1"

6"

ULU KNIFE
TOP VIEW

To download this plan online, go to
makesomething.tv/cuttingboards

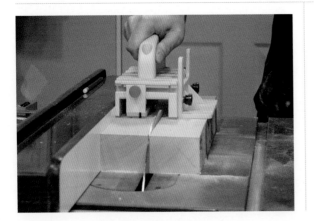

— 1 —

Rip the maple.
For the cutting board, begin by cutting two
maple blanks 2½" wide and 1½" thick at
the tablesaw. For the center section, cut
another piece of maple to 1" x 1½". Then cut
all three pieces to a length of 8".

— 2 —

Prepare the walnut.
To create two contrasting strips of wood for the cutting board, rip two pieces of walnut to ¾" x 1½" and then trim them to 8" long.

— 3 —

Glue up the stock.
Apply a thin layer of glue to all mating faces of the stock and then clamp them up in the pattern shown here.

— 4 —

Flatten it out.
Use a planer to bring the cutting board to uniform thickness. Be sure to take passes on both faces to smooth them out, but leave the stock as thick as possible.

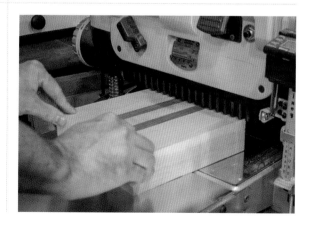

— 5 —

Cut it to size.
At the tablesaw, use a crosscut sled or miter gauge to cut the cutting board to its final dimension of 7½" x 7½".

— 6 —

Prepare to turn.
To mount the cutting board on the lathe, screw the chuck directly to the bottom of the cutting board. Draw lines from corner to corner in both directions to help you center the chuck on the cutting board.

— 7 —

Turn a shallow bowl.
The center should be about ¾" deep and the curve should be of a slightly larger diameter than the knife edge, which will allow the knife to rock back and forth on the board.

Apply a finish.
Feel free to use any food-safe finish.
Here a few coats of mineral oil will be
followed with a few more coats of wax.
For a detailed explanation on finishing
cutting boards see page 156.

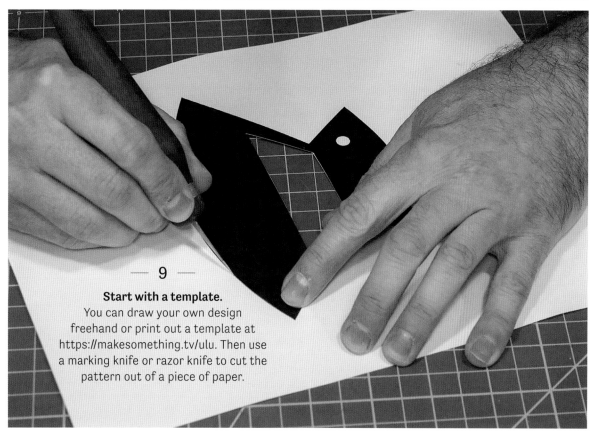

— 9 —

Start with a template.
You can draw your own design
freehand or print out a template at
https://makesomething.tv/ulu. Then use
a marking knife or razor knife to cut the
pattern out of a piece of paper.

— 10 —

Prepare the steel blank.
Apply spray adhesive to the template and then attach it to a piece of 16 gauge stainless steel sheet metal to serve as a stencil. Apply spray paint so the outline can be seen. Remove the template.

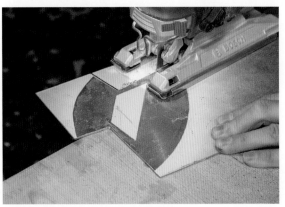

— 11 —

Cut out the steel to shape.
Use a metal-cutting blade in a jigsaw to cut the outer profile of the knife to shape.

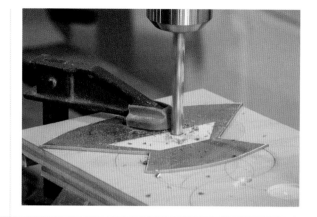

— 12 —

Drill a starter hole.
To saw out the center waste from the blade blank, drill an access hole. Be sure to choose a drill bit slightly larger in diameter than your jigsaw blade.

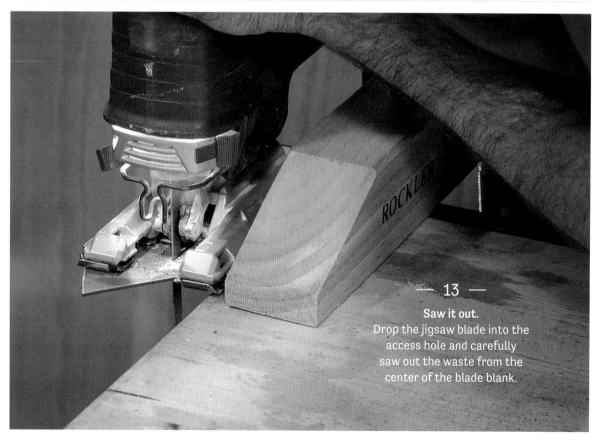

— 13 —

Saw it out.
Drop the jigsaw blade into the access hole and carefully saw out the waste from the center of the blade blank.

— 14 —

Clean it up.
Smooth the edges of the blade blank using a disc sander. You can also use a sheet of sandpaper on a flat surface to smooth the edges — it just takes a little more elbow grease.

— 15 —

Refine the shape.
A belt sander with a narrow belt installed does a good job of reaching the tight corners of the blade blank. Sandpaper and a narrow scrap of wood would work as well.

— 16 —

Smooth the center.
The cutout in the center of the blank is easiest to clean up using a bastard file. Just be sure to clamp the blank securely to your workbench.

17

Make it shine.
The quickest way to bring a polish
to the metal is start sanding with 120 grit
and work your way up to the highest grit
you have. The higher the grit, the
more mirror-like the finish.

18

Soften hard edges.
Rough edges can be smoothed and
slightly rounded using a length of
120-grit sandpaper. It should feel
smooth to the touch.

— 19 —

Mark the bevel.
Use a permanent marker to draw a line about 3/16" from the edge of the blade. This will act as a guide as you shape the bevel.

— 20 —

Rough out the bevel.
Use a belt sander or sandpaper and block to shape the bevel. Be sure not to remove material past the marker line.

— 21 —

Sharpen the knife.
Final sharpening is done using sharpening stones. Waterstones are shown here but oil or ceramic stones would also work. (No sharpening stones? Just use fine, 400–1000 grit wet/dry automotive sandpaper laid over a flat surface.) Begin by flattening the back and then refine the bevel.

— 22 —

Begin the handle.
Resaw a piece of maple down the centerline to create two ½"-thick sides of the knife handle. Other stable hardwoods like ash or walnut would work as well.

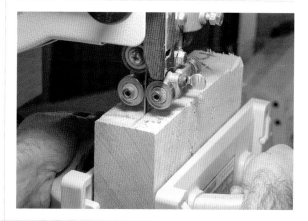

— 23 —

Trace the knife handle.
Draw the outline of the knife handle onto both of the wood blanks.

— 24 —
Cut the handles to shape.
Cut out the handle profile on the two
½"-thick handle blanks. Because you can
sand it to exact shape in a later step,
cut just outside the line.

— 25 —
Glue it up.
Use 5-minute epoxy to glue the
wood handle blanks directly to
each side of the steel blade.

— 26 —
Drill it out.
Once the epoxy dries, drill two ¼" holes
into the handle. Be sure to position the two
holes symmetrically on the handle.

— 27 —

Add the brass rods.
Use epoxy to secure two lengths of ¼"
brass dowel rod into the holes. Brass is
pretty soft and can easily be cut to length
with a hack saw or jigsaw.

— 28 —

Sand everything smooth.
A belt sander makes quick work of sanding
the wood flush with the metal blade.

— 29 —

Put it to work.
The ulu knife rocks back and forth in the
recess of the cutting board, making the pair
as useful as they are handsome.

BRICK END GRAIN

An end grain design with a unique look

TOOLS & SUPPLIES

> Power planer
> Tablesaw
> Clamps
> Drum sander
> Router with 45° chamfer bit
> Random orbit sander
> Glue
> Food-safe finish
> 4 rubber feet with stainless steel screws

MATERIALS

> Vertical "mortar": 4 pieces of hard maple, 1½ x ⅝ x 18-in.
> Horizontal "mortar": 5 pieces of hard maple crosscut and reglued with end grain facing up, 1¼ x ⅝ x 15¾-in.
> "Bricks": 5 pieces of mahogany, 1½ x 3 x 18-in.

After seeing similar designs online, I had to take a stab at building a cutting board with a laid-brick pattern. And subtlety be damned—I went high contrast with mahogany "bricks" and maple "mortar." It's also an end grain design, which means that it doesn't show knife marks.

PLAN

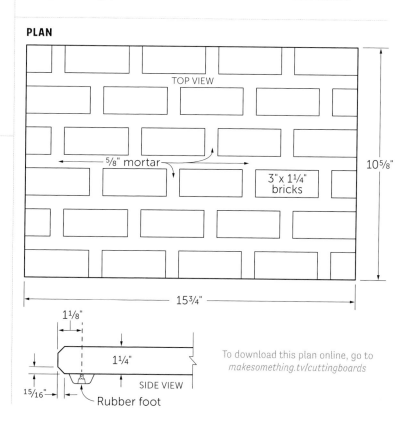

To download this plan online, go to *makesomething.tv/cuttingboards*

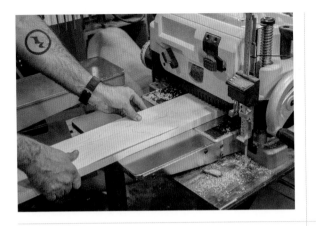

— 1 —
Prepare the "mortar."
Start by planing your hard maple stock to
⅝" thick. The light-colored maple will serve
as the "mortar" of the brick pattern.

— 2 —
Ready the "bricks."
Use mahogany to create the "bricks" for
your cutting board. Begin by planing the
mahogany to 1½" thick. This thickness will
be the height of each brick.

— 3 —
Saw the maple to size.
Rip the maple into 1½"-wide strips
at the tablesaw.

— 4 —
Rip the mahogany.
Because the "bricks" for this cutting board will be 3" long, rip the mahogany to 3" wide at the tablesaw.

— 5 —
Glue it up.
Crosscut all the pieces to about 18" and glue them together. Alternate layers between maple and mahogany as shown in the photo. Spring clamps along the joint lines help keep everything aligned as you tighten the bar clamps across the width.

— 6 —
Level the layers.
Once the glue dries, sand or plane everything smooth. A drum sander works well if you don't want to sand by hand.

— 7 —

Then cut them apart.
You can now rip the board into
1¼"-wide pieces. These cuts determine
the thickness of the cutting board.
You'll need a total of six pieces.

— 8 —

Cut up more "mortar."
Crosscut a length of 1¼"-wide maple
to create the longer "mortar" pieces that
will go between the rows of bricks. Because
you want these pieces to be end grain,
cut a handful to 1¼" wide.

— 9 —

Glue up the maple.

Matching them up edge-to-edge, glue and clamp the maple "mortar" pieces together. You'll need a total of five strips that are 15¾" long.

— 10 —

Flatten the strips.

Once the glue dries on your end grain maple strips, sand them flat using a drum sander or sandpaper secured to a flat surface.

— 11 —

Glue the maple in place.

It's time to glue everything together. Be sure to stagger the brick pieces as shown with the lengths of maple "mortar" positioned between the rows of bricks.

— 12 —

Sand it all again.

Once again, sand everything flush. Having a drum sander for making end grain cutting boards will save you lots of time, but a large flat sanding block and a little elbow grease will work as well.

— 13 —

Square it up.

Using your tablesaw and either a crosscut sled or a miter gauge, square up the ends of the cutting board.

— 14 —

Clean up the edges.

Use a chamfer bit mounted in your handheld router to create a 45° profile on the edges of the top and bottom.

— 15 —

Make everything smooth.
Give both the faces and edges a
final sanding, progressing through finer
and finer grits up to 220 grit.

— 16 —

Apply a finish.
Lay on your favorite food-safe finish.
I used a mix of mineral oil and wax finish
on this board. For more on finishing
cutting boards, see page 156.

— 17 —

Add a few feet.
Attach rubber feet on the bottom
to prevent the board from slipping as
you work. Be sure to use stainless steel
screws to prevent rusting.

KNIFE STORAGE

Convenient design features built-in knife storage

TOOLS & SUPPLIES

> Sliding compound miter saw
> Tablesaw
> Clamps
> Power planer
> Pencil
> Bandsaw
> Combination square
> Spindle sander or sandpaper wrapped around a dowel
> Drill press with
> 3/4- and 3/8-in. Forstner bits
> Mallet
> Flush cut saw
> Random orbit sander
> Sandpaper
> Glue
> 2 knives
> Food-safe finish
> 4 rubber feet with stainless steel screws

This compact workstation has everything you need—a flat, blade-friendly surface for cutting and chopping, and the very knives you need to do it. And because the knives and cutting board are paired, they're always ready to be put to use. This design is created from multiple strips of maple laid out in a pleasing repeating pattern that looks great displayed on your countertop, whether it's in use or not.

MATERIALS

> Cutting board: 15 pieces of maple, $1\frac{1}{2}$ x $\frac{13}{16}$ x $12\frac{1}{4}$-in.
> Top of knife holder: 4 pieces of maple, 1 x $\frac{13}{16}$ x $12\frac{1}{4}$-in.
> Bottom of knife holder: 1 piece of mahogany, $\frac{1}{2}$ x $2\frac{7}{8}$ x $12\frac{1}{4}$-in.
> Large accent dot: 1 mahogany dowel, $\frac{3}{4}$-in. diameter
> Medium accent dot: 1 mahogany dowel, $\frac{1}{2}$-in. diameter
> Small accent dot: 1 mahogany dowel, $\frac{3}{8}$-in. diameter

PLAN

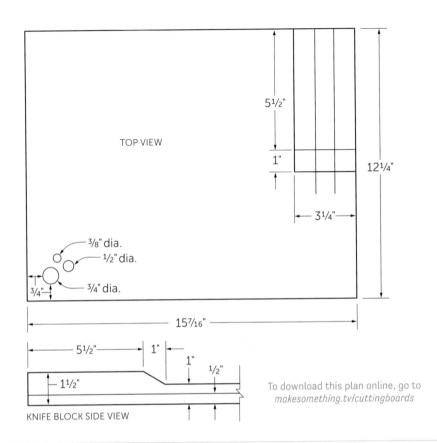

TOP VIEW

5½"

1"

12¼"

3¼"

³⁄₈" dia.

½" dia.

¾" dia.

¾"

15⁷⁄₁₆"

5½"

1"

1"

½"

1½"

KNIFE BLOCK SIDE VIEW

To download this plan online, go to
makesomething.tv/cuttingboards

— 1 —

Break down the stock.

Use a crosscut saw to cut the stock to
length. You'll need enough stock to make up
the full width of the cutting board.

— 2 —
Rip the stock to width.
At the tablesaw, rip the maple cutting board stock to 1½" x ¹³⁄₁₆", and the maple knife holder stock to 1" x ¹³⁄₁₆". When cutting narrow stock, be sure to use a push stick to help guide the boards past the blade.

— 3 —
Glue it up.
Set four pieces of stock aside, then prepare to glue the remaining pieces together face-to-face. Lay a thin layer of glue onto mating faces and secure everything in place with clamps.

— 4 —
Glue up the knife holder.
Glue up the remaining four pieces of stock in the same fashion as the other. This assembly will become the knife block and then attach to the main block.

— 5 —

Thickness the cutting board.
Run both the main block and the knife block
through the thickness planer. To ensure
that both faces are smooth, be sure take
passes on each side of both assemblies.

— 6 —

Draw out the knife handle.
Using your actual knife as a guide, draw
in the recess for the knife handles.
Be sure that the entire length of
the blades will be covered.

— 7 —

Make way for handles.
At the bandsaw, saw away the waste
on the knife block to create a recess to
accommodate the handles.

— 8 —
Layout for the blades.
Use a combination square to mark out equally spaced locations for the two blade slots.

— 9 —
Cut the slots.
At the tablesaw, adjust the fence to make two stopped rip cuts along the layout lines. Once the blade reaches the recess for the handles, hold the stock steady with your push stick and shut off the saw. Don't remove the stock until the blade comes to a full stop.

— 10 —
Smooth it out.
Use a spindle sander or sandpaper wrapped around a dowel to smooth the recess cut for the handle.

— 11 —

Attach a base.
Thickness a piece of mahogany such that its thickness plus the thickness of the knife block equals the thickness of the main cutting board. Then glue and clamp the mahogany to the underside of the knife block.

— 12 —

Trim it to width.
Rip off excess mahogany on both sides of the knife block so that you're left with two smooth edges.

— 13 —

Bring it together.
Add glue to the face of the knife block and the end of the main cutting board and then clamp them together.

— 14 —

Make a clean cut.
Use your tablesaw outfitted with either a miter gauge or a crosscut sled to trim both ends of the cutting board. This will give you nice clean edges on both ends.

— 15 —

Add some bling.
To lend the board visual interest and as a call back to the mahogany set under the knife block, add a few accents with mahogany dowels. In one corner, drill one ¾" hole, one ½", and one ⅜".

— 16 —

Install the dowels.
Add a few drops of glue into each of the holes and drive short lengths of dowel home using a mallet.

— 17 —

Saw it off.
Use a flush cut saw to remove the extra stock on the ends of the dowels.

— 18 —

Smooth it out.
A random orbit sander makes quick work of smoothing the bulk of the cutting board. Work up to 220 grit. Then use handheld sandpaper to soften the corners and smooth the curved recess for the handles.

— 19 —

Give it a glow.
Use a lint-free cotton rag to wipe on your food-safe finish of choice. This board was finished using a combination of mineral oil and wax. For more information on applying food-safe finishes, see page 156.

— 20 —
Install rubber feet.
Once the finish dries, install rubber feet on the bottom of the cutting board. The rubber feet help stabilize the board as you work. To prevent rust, attach the feet using stainless steel screws.

— 21 —
Try it out.
Not only does the cutting board make a handsome addition to your countertop, it's also able and ready for use at any moment.

TABLET HOLDER

Keep your recipe front and center

TOOLS & SUPPLIES

> Sliding compound miter saw
> Tablesaw
> Clamps
> Random orbit sander or drum sander
> Router
> ½-in. bullnose router bit
> 45° chamfer router bit
> Bandsaw
> Glue
> Plywood template
> Food-safe finish
> 4 rubber feet with stainless steel screws

MATERIALS

> Main color: 3 pieces of hickory, ⅞ x 4 x 16-in.
> Accent color and end accents: 4 pieces of mahogany, ⅞ x ¼ x 16-in.
> Tablet holder: 1 piece of hickory, ⅞ x ⅞ x 14¼-in.
> Tablet holder accent: 1 piece of mahogany, ¼ x ⅞ x 14¼-in.

These days it seems like half the meals we cook come from recipes we find online. Or if we're whipping up a favorite old standard, we're often consuming some kind of media while doing so. In either case, I got sick of wiping crumbs and spills off our tablet or phone. But that's a problem no more. The dimensions shown here work with most phones and tablets, but you may need to customize the groove on yours.

PLAN

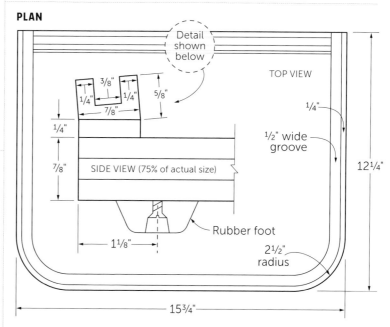

To download this plan online, go to *makesomething.tv/cuttingboards*

— 1 —

Prepare your stock.
Cut 4"-wide hickory to 16" in length.
For a nice, heavy cutting board, each piece
of hickory is ⅞". You'll need a total
of three pieces.

— 2 —

Rip it down.
At the tablesaw, rip ¼" mahogany into
⅞" strips. You'll need a total of four pieces.

— 3 —

Cut the mahogany to length.
Crosscut two of the mahogany strips
to 16" long using either your miter
saw or a tablesaw.

— 4 —
Glue it up.
Glue together three pieces of hickory separated by two pieces of mahogany. Be sure to keep all of the pieces level as you tighten the clamps.

— 5 —
Flatten it out.
Once the glue dries, sand everything flat using a random orbit sander or drum sander.

— 6 —

Square it up.
The two ends of the cutting board can be squared up using a crosscut sled or miter gauge at the tablesaw.

— 7 —

Make room for accents.
Purely for decoration, you can add mahogany strips to the ends of the cutting board. To do so, cut a slot the thickness of the mahogany strips you created in step 2. Use a piece of plywood clamped onto your rip fence to add height and stability as you cut. And be sure to use a push paddle as you cut.

— 8 —

Install the mahogany.
To allow for wood movement, brush a layer of glue on only the center 5" or so of the mahogany strips. Then slide the strips into the grooves and clamp them into place.

— 9 —

Square it up.
Clean up the edges using a crosscut sled or miter gauge at the tablesaw.

— 10 —

Create a juice groove.
Make a plywood template that guides your router ½" inside the perimeter of the cutting board. Remember to round the edges of the template and clamp it in place as you rout the juice groove using a bullnose bit in your router.

— 11 —
Round the corners.
At the bandsaw, round the corners of the cutting board to mirror the curves of the juice groove.

— 12 —
Bevel the bottom.
To help lighten the overall look of the cutting board, use a 45° chamfer bit in a handheld router to chamfer the bottom edge of the cutting board. Position the chamfer so it begins just under the mahogany accent strips on the end.

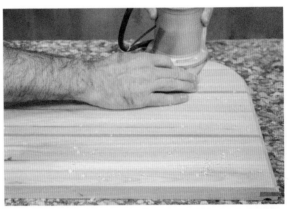

— 13 —
Create a tablet holder.
You may need to customize the tablet holder to work with your particular device—they come in different shapes and sizes and protective cases add additional thickness. For most tablets, a ⅞"-thick piece of hickory cut with a ⅜"-wide groove will work.

— 14 —

Let it lean.
Tilt your blade a few degrees and cut
an angle on the bottom of the tablet holder.
This will allow the tablet to sit at an angle,
making it easier to read while using
the cutting board.

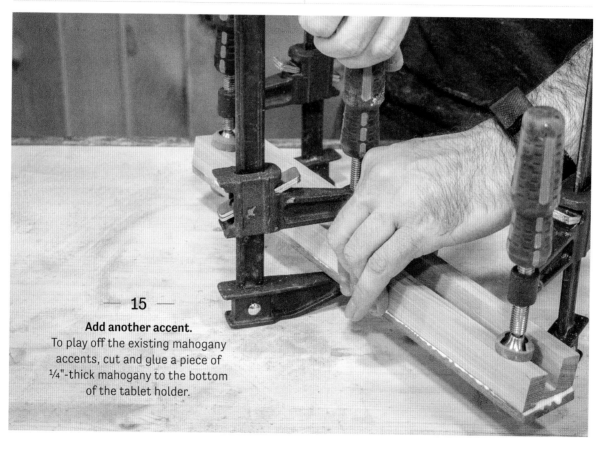

— 15 —

Add another accent.
To play off the existing mahogany
accents, cut and glue a piece of
¼"-thick mahogany to the bottom
of the tablet holder.

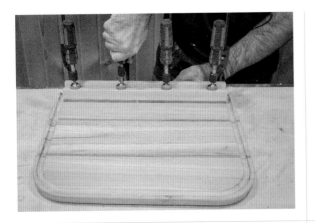

— 16 —

Add the holder.
Cut the tablet holder to fit between the two juice grooves and glue it into place.

— 17 —

Clean up the edge.
Flush up the rear edge of the cutting board by making a rip cut at the tablesaw.

— 18 —

Smooth it out.
Sand everything smooth to 220 grit, using a combination of working with a random orbit sander and hand sanding.

— 19 —
Lay on the finish.
Lay on a few coats of your favorite food-safe finish. For more on finishing cutting boards, see page 156.

— 20 —
Install the feet.
Predrill and screw in rubber feet to the bottom of the cutting board. Be sure to use stainless steel screws to prevent rust.

To see a video of this design being built, go to *makesomething.tv*.

CUTTING BOARD
INLAY

A beautiful design element made easy

TOOLS & SUPPLIES

› Sliding compound miter saw
› Tablesaw
› Pencil
› Screws
› MDF for template
› Bandsaw
› Random orbit sander
› Clamps
› Router with ¼-in. straight bit and 45° chamfer bit
› Router table with flush trim bit
› Handplane
› Disc sander or sandpaper
› Glue
› Food-safe finish
› 4 rubber feet with stainless steel screws

Cutting boards make the perfect excuse to try new things and experiment with new materials and techniques. This is a smart method for inlay that I picked up from an article by Scott Lewis in *Fine Woodworking* magazine a few years ago, but the same technique could be applied to a tabletop or door panel. And once you break this method down into steps, it's actually very simple. For looks, durability, and stability, I built this board using bamboo plywood.

MATERIALS

› Cutting board: 1 piece of bamboo plywood, ¾ x 12 x 18-in.
› Inlay edges: 2 pieces of Mexican ebony, ¾ x $\frac{1}{16}$ x 20-in.
› Inlay center: 1 piece of mahogany, ¾ x ⅛ x 20-in. (The width should be sized so the entire inlay piece is ¼-in. wide)

PLAN

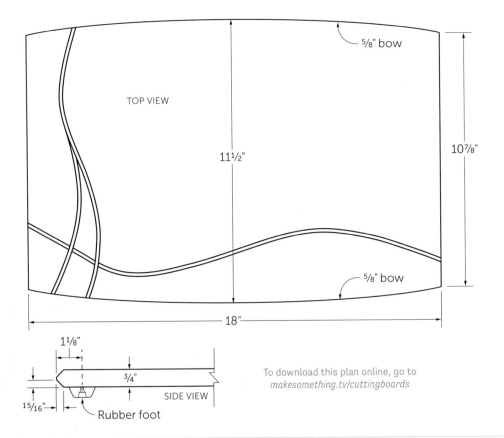

TOP VIEW

⁵⁄₈" bow

10⁷⁄₈"

11½"

18"

⁵⁄₈" bow

1⅛"

¾"

SIDE VIEW

15⁄16"

Rubber foot

To download this plan online, go to
makesomething.tv/cuttingboards

— 1 —

Rough out the stock.
This design is made using 12"-wide,
¾"-thick bamboo. Start by
crosscutting it to 18" long.

— 2 —
Create the inlay materials.
This board is inlaid using very thin strips of Mexican ebony, but any hardwood that contrasts with the bamboo would work as well.

— 3 —
Add a layer.
Adding a strip of mahogany between the Mexican ebony works well with the bamboo. It's important that the inlay equals the thickness of your router bit (step 7). I'll be using a ¼"-wide straight bit so my three pieces of inlay add up to ¼". Size the mahogany strips accordingly.

— 4 —
Draw the curve.
To rout the curves into the bamboo you'll need a template. All you need is piece of MDF, screws, and a piece of veneer or thin strip of wood. Adjust as necessary to draw curves that seem pleasing to your eye.

— 5 —
Cut out the shape.
To create the template, cut out the
curve on the bandsaw. Do your
best to split the line as you cut.

— 6 —
Fair the curves.
The curves should be as smooth as possible.
Use a sander, rasp, or sandpaper
wrapped around a block to remove
any bumps or blade marks.

— 7 —
Cut the groove.
With your template clamped to the top of the bamboo, rout a ¼" groove roughly one-third as deep as the bamboo is thick. As you work, make sure the baseplate on the router rides against the template throughout the cut.

— 8 —
Saw through the groove.
Cut the stock into two pieces at the bandsaw. Make sure your blade follows the groove left by the router.

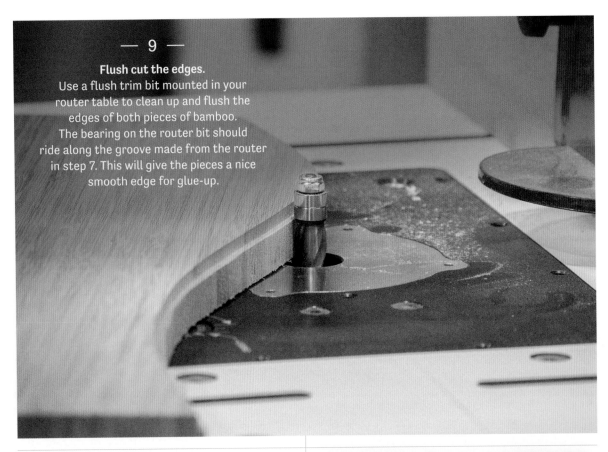

— 9 —

Flush cut the edges.
Use a flush trim bit mounted in your router table to clean up and flush the edges of both pieces of bamboo. The bearing on the router bit should ride along the groove made from the router in step 7. This will give the pieces a nice smooth edge for glue-up.

— 10 —

Bring it all together.
Lay on a thin layer of glue between all mating edges — both the two pieces of bamboo and three pieces of veneer. Then use clamps to bring the assembly together. This glue-up can be tricky; tighten the clamps slowly and make sure your veneers protrude both above and below the surface.

— 11 —
Clean up the veneer.
Use a handplane to trim away the
excess veneer and flatten both sides
of the cutting board.

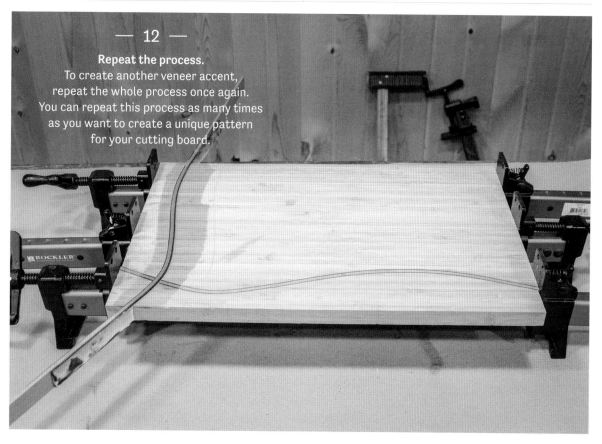

— 12 —
Repeat the process.
To create another veneer accent,
repeat the whole process once again.
You can repeat this process as many times
as you want to create a unique pattern
for your cutting board.

— 13 —

Complete the design.
The pattern seen here took three templates, three sets of veneer, and three glue-ups.

— 14 —

Square it up.
Once everything is dry and sanded, square up the ends of the cutting board using a miter gauge on your tablesaw.

— 15 —

Draw out a curve.
To create a pleasing curve along the top and bottom, bend a a piece of leftover veneer — or thin stock of any kind — and draw in the line.

— 16 —

Cut out the curve.
Back at the bandsaw, follow the guideline to cut out the curves on both the top and bottom edges of the cutting board.

— 17 —

Smooth the edges.
The bandsaw can leave rough cutlines, which you can sand away by hand or using a disc sander.

— 18 —
Ease the edges.
Use a handheld router outfitted with
a 45° chamfer bit to knock the hard edges
off both the top and bottom of the cutting
board. If you prefer a rounded edge, choose
a roundover bit instead.

— 19 —
Smooth it out.
Use a random orbit sander to
sand the faces and edges. Progress
up to 220 grit before finishing.

— 20 —

Apply a finish.
Rub on your favorite finish using a lint-free cotton rag. For more on choosing and using food-safe finishes, check out page 156.

— 21 —

Add rubber feet.
To prevent the cutting board from sliding around as you work, attach rubber feet to the bottom using stainless steel screws.

CHOOSING & USING FOOD-SAFE FINISHES

There are many ways to finish a cutting board and no finish is maintenance free. The more you use the cutting board, the more you'll need to apply more finish. The finish I like to use takes a two-step process. The first step is applying mineral oil that seeps deep into the wood, and the second step adds a protective film on top of the surface.

Lumber Choice Comes First

When choosing woods for cutting boards, look for dense hardwoods, as they are more durable and can stand up to kitchen tasks. You should also lean toward woods that don't contain an excess of natural oils. Some people have a sensitivity to these oils, and you don't want your cutting board to alter the taste of your food.

Most people also stay away from spalted and reclaimed woods because you don't always know what you're dealing with. If you do use spalted or reclaimed woods, be sure to seal the surface so that it won't affect the food in any way.

In general, North American hardwoods like maple, walnut, and cherry are commonly used in cutting boards, and rare exotic woods should be avoided. Whatever woods you choose, do your research on food safety before venturing into the unknown.

1

1 Start with smooth stock. Sand everything down to 220 grit. A good sanding job pays off well on small jobs that beg to be touched.

2 Raise the grain. Use a wet paper towel to raise the grain. The moisture causes some of the wood fibers to swell.

3 Remove the raised grain. Go back and sand everything smooth again with 220-grit sandpaper. This second sanding won't take long to smooth everything back out. This step will keep the cutting board smooth after use and washing.

4 Lay on the oil. Coat the entire cutting board with a heavy dose of white, food-grade mineral oil.

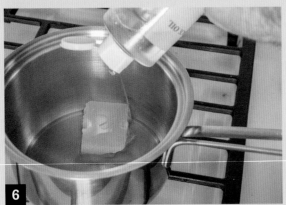

5 And again . . . Some woods and all end grain cutting boards soak up a lot of mineral oil. Keep applying more and more until the oil sits on the surface. Allow the oil to sit for a couple of hours before wiping away any excess.

6 Add a little wax. For the second coat, melt paraffin wax on the stove using the lowest heat setting. As the wax melts add a bit of the white, food-grade mineral oil. You'll want about a 50/50 mix.

7 Finish while it's hot. While the wax mixture is still warm, apply a heavy coat to the cutting board. Let the wax set for a couple of hours. This will leave a film on the surface but it's easily removed later.

8 Buff it out. Use a soft cloth to buff away the wax. This coat gives your cutting board a protective finish and a satin sheen.

8

≫ **Richard Boudoin**
Katy, Texas, USA

CUTTING BOARD

GALLERY

Attention, cutting board builders . . .

Followers of Make Something were asked to submit photos
of their own cutting board projects. Response was quick
and impressive, representing a wide range of designs—
from elegant and simple to technical wonders. From the
many submissions received, these were among our favorites.

⌃ **Austin Greenway**
Mountain Home, Idaho, USA

≫ **Tom Pritchard**
Madison, Indiana, USA

≫ **Josh Price**
Kingsland, Georgia, USA

≫ **Coenraad van Tonder**
Bloemfontein, Free State, South Africa

≫ **Leroy Aldinger**
Overland Park, Kansas, USA

⌃ **Daniel Kasprick**
Goddard, Kansas, USA

⌃ **Derek Goss**
Atascadero, California, USA

⌃ **Leroy Aldinger**
Overland Park, Kansas, USA

⌃ **Christopher Tucker**
Denver, Colorado, USA

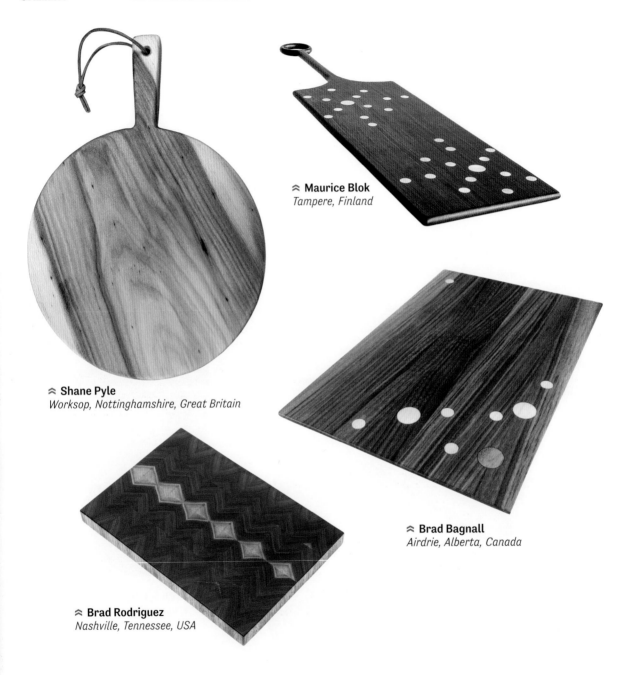

≫ Maurice Blok
Tampere, Finland

≫ Shane Pyle
Worksop, Nottinghamshire, Great Britain

≫ Brad Bagnall
Airdrie, Alberta, Canada

≫ Brad Rodriguez
Nashville, Tennessee, USA

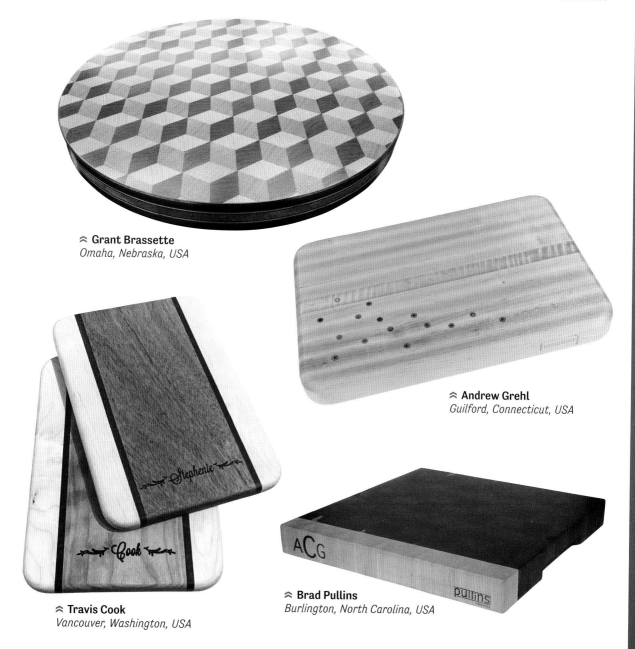

⌃ **Grant Brassette**
Omaha, Nebraska, USA

⌃ **Andrew Grehl**
Guilford, Connecticut, USA

⌃ **Travis Cook**
Vancouver, Washington, USA

⌃ **Brad Pullins**
Burlington, North Carolina, USA

≫ **Chris Thomas**
Fremont, California, USA

≫ **Con Papandonis**
Sydney, New South Wales, Australia

≫ **Joseph Muench**
Las Cruces, New Mexico, USA

≫ **Patrick Sinn**
Iowa City, Iowa, USA

ACKNOWLEDGEMENTS

I wouldn't be able to do what I do without the help from people like you who purchase these books, watch my videos, and follow me on social media. I'd like to give a special thanks to those who donate their hard-earned money every month on Patreon. If you would like to learn how you can help support me visit https://www.patreon.com/picciuto to find out more.

My top Patreon supporters. . .

Nathan Bird, Renae Sanders, Kevin Fitzpatrick, Allen Sparks, Chris Vincent, Brett Yerks, Alex Dulwick, Aaron Stoddart, Nicholas Gomez, Rick Carkin, Joseph Muench, Tom Reagh, William Benton, Joshua Ripley, Matt Walker, Green Hill Graphics, Luis Gonzalez, Steve Hay, Chris Killingsworth, Rick Smith, David Plance, Gabriel Sentiff, James McIlhargey, Patrick Boulanger, John Hankins, Adam Thomason, Victor Ludick, Taylor Martin, Jake Almer, Jay Hilgeford, Stephen Caperton, Mat Jones, Jason Brown, Robert Rittenhouse, Justin Herman, Manhattan Wood Project, Peter Metzger, Joseph Foster, Loke Alexander Vikne, David L Williams, Scott Underwood, Zachary Wolfrom, Kyle C Quinn, Andrew Fischer, Tom Kelly, Daniel Kiviaho, Allen Canterbury, Jim Rumsey, Gerald Downing, John Kelly, Carl Brink, Brad Hubbard, David Miller, Dustin Null, Mickey Griffith, Arthur Ball, Benjamin Keller, Jason Evans, Ken Weinert, Joey Sawyer, Ryan Parish, Dee Perez, Stephen Huff, Elijah Taylor, James R (Rob) Casey, Scott Burdick, Christian Simonsen, Ben Zarges, I Like To Make Stuff, David Hess, Nick Whitworth, Leif Johnson, David Dyess, Sam Brelsfoard, Jonathan Van Vuren, Dan Nolan, Doug Hesseltine, Jason Smith, Brian Gillman, Jared Ross, Bryce Stoddart, Jeremy Wassink, Filippe F Guimaraes, Eric Penewell, Jens Rosemeyer, Brad Bell, Majid Al Qassimi, Brad Dudenhoffer, Brian Prusa, Bradley Lindseth, Fix This Build That, Anthony Procacci, Tom, Tyler Faruque, Bas Bruininkx, Whitten Schulz, Jason Hughes, Chris Collins, Matt Danner, Maker Playground, Jesse Hughson, Matt Kummell, Lucien Lasocki, Kelly Burns, Sam Blaydon, Troy Brown, Jason Adamczyk, Mark, Joshua Smith, Charles Hartwell, Margaret Lanaghan, Brian Elia, Woodworking Geek, Will Work For Tools, Eric Anderson, Matthew Arns, Jeff Holden, Keith Ketcham, Spoonless Corey, JC's Wood Works, Gus Thomas, Dave Mclean, Paul Brickley, Daniel Rodriguez, Robert Perkins, Jared Thomas, David Murray, Blake Alexander, Russel Clites, Kevin Brewer, Howard Springsteen, Wayne Timbers, Miter Mike's Woodshop, Jim Ashley, Rene Sørensen, David Russell, Michael Schubert, Paul Michael Kane, Greg Karnow, Tom Pritchard, Kevin Blank, Andrew McGaugh, J.P. Drew, Larry Edens, Justin Capogna, Jesse DiMura, Ben Martens, Justin D. Morgan, Travis Cook, Austin McKimmey, Joel Pepin, Gerald Braun, Donald Powell, Brian Shannon, Luke Binezar, Rick Miller, Chet Kloss, Nick Ryan, Michael Schuler, Bradley Jeffers, Jack A Helm, Paul Stordy, Ben Vogelsang, Andrew Jones, Martin Saban-Smith, Bruce A. Ulrich, Matthew Chudy, Joe Pierce, JM Tosses, Ryan Bailey, James Rice, David Macauley, Eric Burke, Rob Leno Jr., Reviewy McReviewface, Chase Vincent, Daniel Richard, Paul Rothrock, Tanel Eiskop, Timothy Xil, Colin Bodor, Dylan Parker, Scott Bruce, Philippe Majerus, John Glass, Gareth Crispin, Petr Tošovský, Kit Hygh, Laura Kampf, Zach Spille, Shawn Livingston, Mike Greene, Thomas Desor, Ashley Stillson, Rich Alix

INDEX

Note: *Italics* indicate projects.

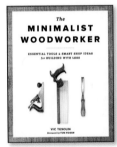
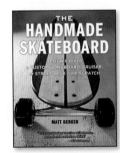